Peru

Many Cultures,
One World

by Barbara Knox

Consultant:
Dr. Thomas A. Brown
Professor of Latin American History
Augustana College
Rock Island, Illinois

Blue Earth Books

an imprint of Capstone Press
Mankato, Minnesota

Blue Earth Books are published by Capstone Press
151 Good Counsel Drive, P.O. Box 669, Mankato, Minnesota 56002
http://www.capstonepress.com

Library of Congress Cataloging-in-Publication Data
Knox, Barbara.
　　Peru / by Barbara Knox.
　　p. cm. — (Many cultures, one world)
　　Includes bibliographical references and index.
　　Contents: Welcome to Peru—A Peruvian legend—City and country life—Seasons in Peru—Family life in Peru—Laws, rules,
and customs—Pets in Peru—Sights to see in Peru.
　　ISBN 0-7368-2450-2 (hardcover)
　　1. Peru—Juvenile literature. [1. Peru.] I. Title. II. Series.
F3408.5.K66 2004
985—dc22
2003012126

Editorial credits

Editor: Megan Schoeneberger
Series Designer: Kia Adams
Photo Researcher: Alta Schaffer
Product Planning Editor: Eric Kudalis

Cover photo of Machu Picchu by Corbis

Artistic effects
Rubberball

1 2 3 4 5 6 09 08 07 06 05 04

Photo credits

Betty Crowell, 4–5
Blaine Harrington III, 20
Bruce Coleman Inc./Erwin and Peggy Bauer, 27 (right)
Capstone Press/Gary Sundermeyer, 3 (all), 15, 21, 25, back cover
Corbis/Alison Wright, 28–29; Lloyd Cluff, 9 (right); Michael and
　　Patricia Fogden, 29 (right)
Cory Langley, 16, 26
Doranne Jacobson, 19 (right), 24
Getty Images Inc., 23
Houserstock/Dave G. Houser, 14; Michael J. Pettypool, 12–13;
　　Rankin Harvey, 6
James P. Rowan, 8–9, 10
Michele Burgess, 11, 13 (right), 18–19, 27 (left)
One Mile Up Inc., 22 (top)
Pete and Jill Yearneau, 22 (bottom)
TRIP/M. Jelliffe, 17

Contents

Check out page 15 to find out how to weave a paper mat.

Turn to page 7 to find a map of Peru.

Look on page 21 to learn how to make a Peruvian dessert.

See page 25 to learn how to play a Peruvian game called *sapo*.

CHAPTER 1

Welcome to Peru

Machu Picchu, Peru's city in the clouds, sits high in the mountains. Clouds hang like fog around the very old city. Machu Picchu means "old peak." Steep stairs lead to hundreds of crumbling stone buildings.

Inca Indians built the city in the 1400s. In the 1500s, Spanish explorers took control of the land around Machu Picchu. The Incas left the city. Machu Picchu was forgotten until it was found again in 1911.

The ruins of Machu Picchu, an ancient Incan city, include many terraces built into the side of the mountain.

Facts about Peru

Name:................Republic of Peru
Capital:..............Lima
Population:.........28 million people
Size:...................496,224 square miles
                      (1,285,220 square kilometers)
Languages:.........Spanish, Quechua
Religion:............Roman Catholic (90 percent),
                      other (10 percent)
Highest point: ....Mount Huascarán, 22,205 feet
                      (6,768 meters)
Lowest point:.....Pacific Ocean, sea level
Main crops: ....Potatoes, sugarcane,
                      coffee, cotton
Money:..............*Nuevo sol*

Today, visitors climb the ruins to explore. Green valleys surround the city. Far off, other mountain peaks rise to the clouds.

Peru has mountains, deserts, and **rain forests**. Peru's desert coast on the Pacific Ocean is one of the driest places on Earth. The tall Andes Mountains stretch from north to south. The mountains have clear lakes and snow-covered peaks. Farther east, rain forests cover most of the country. The Amazon River flows through this area. At about 4,000 miles (6,400 kilometers), it is the largest river in South America. Many smaller rivers flow into the Amazon.

Peru is South America's third largest country. It is about the same size as the state of Alaska.

The rain forests of eastern Peru are thick with plant life, such as palms, ferns, and giant lily pads.

Map of Peru

COLOMBIA

ECUADOR

Amazon River

Iquitos ●

BRAZIL

P E R U

Trujillo ●

P A C I F I C
O C E A N

A n d e s   M o u n t a i n s

◆ *Mount Huascarán*

Lima ✪

▬ MACHU PICCHU

● Cuzco

BOLIVIA

Lake Titicaca

Legend

✪ Capital City
● City
◆ Highest Point
▬ Landmark
⛰ Mountain Range
〜 River

Arequipa ●

N
W   E
S

CHILE

7

CHAPTER 2

A Peruvian Legend

Peru has many floods. Huge waves called **tsunamis** sometimes rise from the ocean. The waves crash into the coast. Other times, rainstorms drown the land.

People around the world tell stories and legends of a flood that once covered the Earth. In Peru's flood story, a **llama** warns people and animals before the flood. Mexicans tell of a bird that warns of an upcoming flood. In the Bible, a man named Noah brings two of every kind of animal onto his boat. They float in the boat until they are safe.

People who live along Peru's rivers often live in houses built on stilts. The houses are safe when heavy rains cause floods.

Floods sometimes reach the rooftops of people's houses. Water can cover an entire city.

Llamas are important to the people of Peru. Many families use llamas to carry loads through the mountains. They also use the llamas' wool for weaving.

Peruvians treat their llamas with great care. They tie bells and ribbons around their llamas' necks. They find the best grass for the llamas to eat. Men play flutes for the llamas while they eat. They believe the music calms the animals so they do not run off.

A man plays music on a wooden flute. Llama herders believe the quiet music calms their llamas.

The Llama and the Flood

Long ago, a llama lived with a farmer's family in the mountains. The llama helped the farmer carry large loads. The llama enjoyed eating. It often stopped to snack on grass along the path.

One day, the llama did not want to eat. The farmer tried for five days to feed it. On the fifth day, the farmer begged the llama to eat. He did not want his llama to die.

To the farmer's surprise, the llama began to cry. The llama told the farmer that the ocean was changing. It would soon flood the land. They should climb to the top of the highest mountain.

The farmer believed his llama. The family loaded their belongings onto the llama. Together, they began to climb. As the group climbed, the llama warned other animals about the flood. Flamingos, pumas, **chinchillas**, and foxes joined the group.

Water rose around the mountain, touching the foxes' tails. The sun disappeared. The world became cold. Suddenly, the sun came out again. It dried the land. The water went down. The llama, the farmer's family, and the animals were safe. They climbed down the mountain together.

The llama in the story helped lead the farmer and his family into the mountains and away from danger.

CHAPTER 3

City and Country Life

Most of Peru's cities are near the coast. Many people live in Arequipa, Trujillo, and Lima.

Lima is Peru's largest city. It is a little smaller than New York City. More than 7 million people live in Lima. It has museums, colleges, and high-rise office buildings.

Many Peruvians come to cities to work. They build houses, apartments, and other buildings. Other people make clothing or machine parts in factories. In Lima, some people work for the national government.

People fill the streets of Lima. Lima and other large Peruvian cities have many businesses and shops.

Floating Homes

At Lake Titicaca, a small group of Uros Indians lives on floating islands. They use bundles of tall grass to make the islands. They use more grass to build boats and small houses.

13

Many people in Peru are very poor. They do not have enough money to buy houses in the city. They live in small apartments.

Some people cannot even pay for apartments. They use cardboard and scraps of wood to build homes near cities. They have no running water or electricity.

Other Peruvians live in small villages in the Andes Mountains. These people grow potatoes, corn, wheat, and a grain called quinoa. They raise sheep, llamas, guinea pigs, and other animals. They live in mud brick homes with grass roofs.

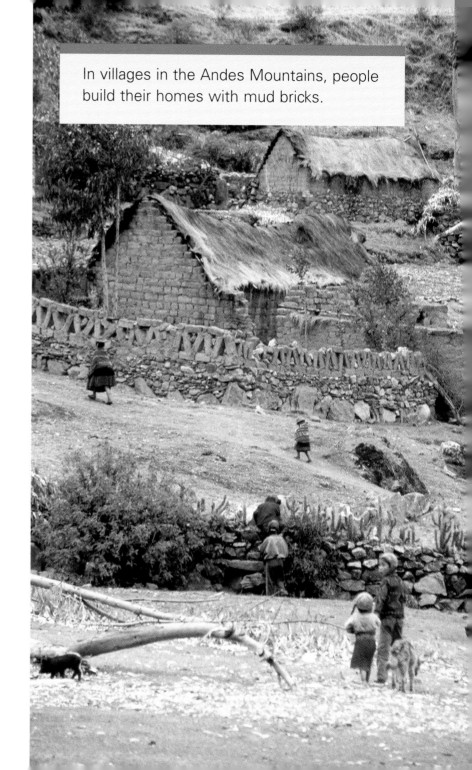

In villages in the Andes Mountains, people build their homes with mud bricks.

Weave a Paper Mat

For thousands of years, Peruvians in the Andes Mountains have made cloth by hand. Today, they still make yarn from llama, **alpaca**, and sheep wool. They dye the yarn bright colors with berries and plants. They use a loom to weave patterns into the cloth. The patterns stand for mountains, rivers, and animals. You can make a paper mat using the same over-and-under method that Peruvian weavers use.

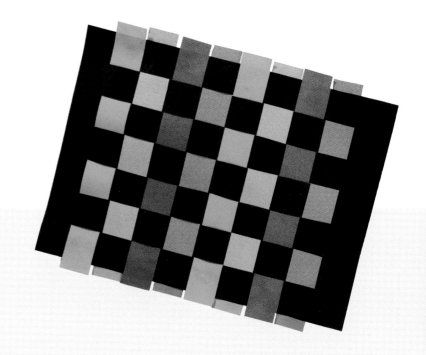

What You Need

pieces of construction paper in different colors
ruler
scissors
glue

What You Do

1. Fold one piece of paper in half lengthwise. Use the ruler to draw a line about 1 inch (2.5 centimeters) from the open edge. Make several cuts from the folded edge up to the line. Open the paper.
2. From the other pieces of paper, cut about eight long, narrow strips.
3. Push one strip of paper under and over the cuts made in the first paper. Push a second strip of paper over and under the cuts. Weave in and out of the paper with all your strips.
4. To finish the edges of your mat, glue the ends of the strips in place.

CHAPTER 4

Seasons in Peru

Peru's seasons are almost opposite of those in North America. In Peru, summer starts in January. Winter begins in May. Summers are often rainy. Winters are sunny and dry. Most people in Peru just call their two seasons wet and dry.

Peru's desert runs along the coast. In the south, children can ride down tall sand dunes on sandboards. Sandboards are similar to snowboards.

Only cactus and small bushes grow in dry areas of Peru.

Farther north near Lima, the weather is very unusual. Even though the desert area is very dry, the air feels damp and sticky in summer. For the rest of the year, fog hangs in the cloudy, gray sky.

In the mountains, the weather is usually hot and sunny. Higher in the mountains, winter weather can be cold. Summers can be rainy.

Rain forests cover eastern Peru. In the rain forest, rainfall is measured in feet, not inches (meters, not centimeters). From January to April, roads turn into muddy streams. The warm sunlight turns the moisture into steam.

Peru's coastal desert has large sand dunes.

CHAPTER 5

Family Life in Peru

Peruvian families live close together. Grandparents, parents, children, uncles, aunts, and cousins sometimes share the same home. The Quechua Indians in the mountains live in smaller homes. Still, relatives usually live in the same village.

Family life for poor Peruvians is not like North American life. TVs and stereos are not common in Peruvian homes. In the cities, both parents sometimes work 12 hours a day to earn money for food. Older children help care for their younger brothers and sisters.

Quechua Indian girls learn the art of weaving by watching their mothers weave.

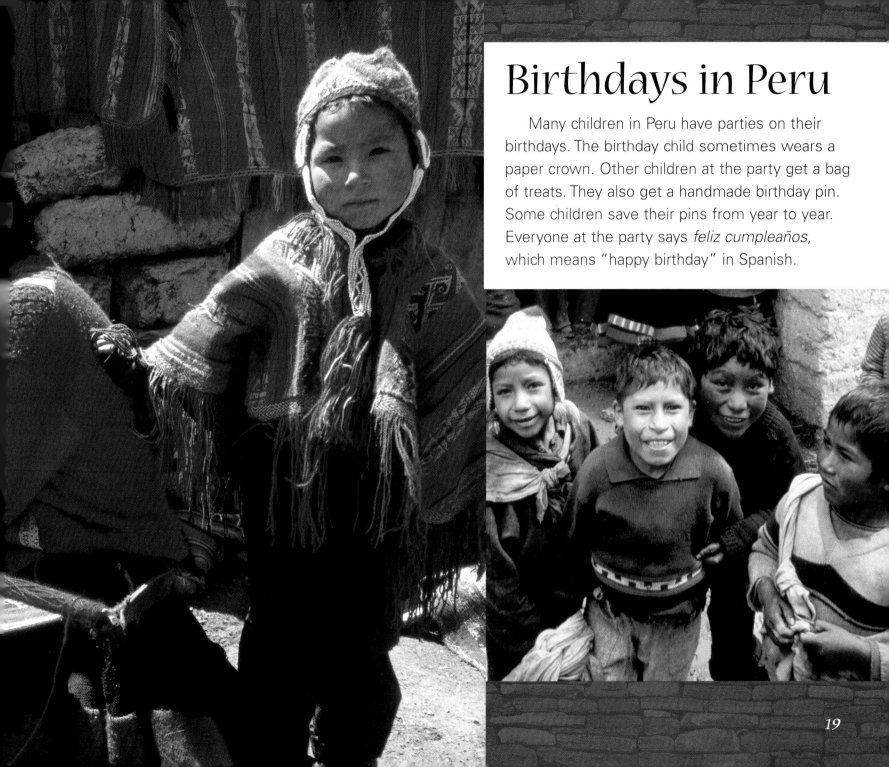

Birthdays in Peru

Many children in Peru have parties on their birthdays. The birthday child sometimes wears a paper crown. Other children at the party get a bag of treats. They also get a handmade birthday pin. Some children save their pins from year to year. Everyone at the party says *feliz cumpleaños*, which means "happy birthday" in Spanish.

19

Families with more money enjoy many of the same activities as North Americans. They watch TV, see movies, and play soccer and other sports.

Almost all Peruvians are Roman Catholic. Roman Catholics follow the teachings of Jesus Christ. Their leader, the pope, lives in Rome.

Peruvians across the country celebrate Easter week. In Lima, the people parade through the streets with candles. Wax drips from their candles, making the streets slippery.

People in Peru eat potatoes at almost every meal. More than 2,000 kinds of potatoes grow in Peru. Potatoes are often mixed with meat and other vegetables and served over rice. Peruvians also eat cold potatoes, dried potatoes, and potato soup.

Some families in the cities live in large houses with private gardens and patios.

Rice Pudding

Peruvians love rice pudding, or *arroz con leche.* Many restaurants in the larger cities offer this creamy dessert. Peruvians like to serve the pudding to visitors. You can eat it warm or cold. To make it even sweeter, add a little cinnamon and sugar.

What You Need

Ingredients

½ cup (120 mL) short- or
    medium-grain rice
2 cups (480 mL) milk
1 stick cinnamon
2 tablespoons (30 mL)
    sugar
½ cup (120 mL) raisins
1 apple, peeled, cut,
    and diced
optional toppings:
    cinnamon and sugar

Equipment

medium saucepan with lid
liquid measuring cup
measuring spoons
dry-ingredient measuring
    cups
mixing spoon

What You Do

1. In a saucepan, combine rice, milk, cinnamon stick, sugar, raisins, and apple pieces.
2. Heat until mixture comes to a boil.
3. Reduce heat to low. Cover saucepan with lid.
4. Cook until the milk is absorbed, about 45 to 60 minutes.
5. Remove the cinnamon stick.
6. Serve warm or chill and serve cold.
7. Sprinkle with cinnamon and sugar or add an apple slice before serving, if desired.

Makes 4 to 6 servings

CHAPTER 6

Laws, Rules, and Customs

Peru declared its freedom from Spain in 1821. The country celebrates Independence Day every year on July 28. People go to parades and parties called fiestas.

Peru's government is a **democracy**. Every five years, people vote for a president. Peru's congress meets in Lima. The congress works with the president to make Peru's laws.

Peru's laws require children to go to school from age 6 through 16. The government runs most schools. Some families in the cities pay to send their children to private schools.

Peru's flag is red with a white stripe down the middle. Peru's coat of arms sits in the middle of the white stripe. The coat of arms shows an animal called a **vicuña**, a tree, and gold coins spilling out of a basket. The pictures stand for Peru's wildlife, plants, and **minerals**. Peru began using its flag in 1825.

Peru's money is called the *nuevo sol*. One *nuevo sol* is worth 100 *céntimos*, or cents.

In Peru, people vote for the president in national elections.

23

Peruvians living in small villages know that having a school is very important. Villagers often build their own schools if the government has not built one. At all schools, children learn to read and write Spanish.

In small villages, children share desks and school supplies.

Sapo

Many Peruvians play a game called *sapo*. According to a legend, a king's family once threw gold pieces into Lake Titicaca. If a frog caught the gold, it would bring good luck.

To play *sapo*, players toss brass pieces at a wooden box. The box has holes in the top. Players win points depending on which hole the piece falls into. The player with the most points wins the game. You can make your own *sapo* game to practice your aim.

What You Need

two or more players
small muffin tin
self-adhesive number stickers
ruler
12 buttons for each player

What You Do

1. Assign points to each cup of the muffin tin by attaching self-adhesive number stickers. You can use any number of points you like, but make sure each cup has a different number of points.
2. Stand back about 2 feet (.6 meter) from the muffin tin and toss a button toward it. Try to get the button to land inside a cup. Keep tossing until you have used all 12 buttons.
3. Add up your points for any buttons that landed inside the cup.
4. The other players take their turns, following the directions above.
5. Once everyone has had a turn, the player with the most points wins the game.

CHAPTER 7

Pets in Peru

Peruvians take good care of their pet dogs. Dog owners feed their dogs bits of table food rather than dog food.

In poorer areas, stray dogs usually belong to the whole area. No one family owns a dog. All of the families work together taking care of these dogs.

Indians in the Andes Mountains treat their llamas and alpacas like pets. Alpacas are similar to llamas, but they have longer wool. Llamas and alpacas are very gentle. Indians use these animals to carry large loads through the mountains.

Some children in Peru's cities have pet dogs.

Children treat their llamas like pets.

Chinchillas

Chinchillas are small, furry rodents. These animals live in the Andes Mountains. Indians used the chinchilla's very soft fur to make clothing and bedcovers. In the early 1900s, 11 chinchillas were caught and sent to the United States. Today, chinchillas are popular pets in the United States.

CHAPTER 8

Sights to See in Peru

Many Peruvian cities show off beautiful buildings. In Trujillo, fancy gates surround huge homes. Arequipa has many white stone buildings. People call it the white city. Cuzco has very old stone walls and buildings built by the Inca Indians.

Iquitos is the largest city in the rain forest. The only way to get to Iquitos is by plane or boat. Around the city, trees grow tall and thick. Sunlight cannot reach the ground. Near Iquitos, hanging bridges cross the treetops. People sometimes see snakes or flashes of colorful butterflies and parrots.

Hanging bridges lead people through the rain forest near Iquitos, Peru.

Colpas

Visitors often come to large cliffs of red clay called *colpas* to see many kinds of parrots. Hundreds, sometimes thousands, of birds come to the *colpas* each day. Each morning and evening, they eat the clay. The bright red, green, blue, and yellow birds hang on the side of the cliff. The birds make a noisy wall of color.

Glossary

alpaca (al-PAK-uh)—a South American animal that is related to the camel and the llama; alpacas have long, silky wool.

chinchilla (chin-CHIL-uh)—a small South American rodent with silvery-gray fur

democracy (de-MOK-ruh-see)—a type of government where people vote for their leaders

llama (LAH-muh)—a South American animal raised for its wool and used to carry loads; the llama is related to the camel and the alpaca.

mineral (MIN-ur-uhl)—a substance found in nature that is not an animal or a plant; copper, silver, and gold are minerals found in Peru.

rain forest (RAYN FOR-ist)—a dense forest where much rain falls

tsunami (tsoo-NAH-mee)—a very large wave caused by an underwater earthquake or volcano

vicuña (vih-KOON-yah)—a wild animal from South America that is related to the camel and the llama; vicuñas are in danger of dying out.

Read More

Cavan, Seamus. *Peru.* Steadwell Books World Tour. Austin, Texas: Raintree Steck-Vaughn, 2002.

Fajardo, Sara Andrea. *In a Peruvian City.* A Child's Day. New York: Benchmark Books, 2003.

Lassieur, Allison. *Peru.* Countries and Cultures. Mankato, Minn.: Capstone Press, 2003.

Useful Addresses

Embassy of Peru—Canada
130 Albert Street, Suite 1901
Ottawa, ON K1P 5G4
Canada

Embassy of Peru—United States
1700 Massachusetts Avenue NW
Washington, DC 20036

Peabody Museum of Natural History
Yale University
P.O. Box 208118
170 Whitney Avenue
New Haven, CT 06520-8118

Internet Sites

FactHound offers a safe, fun way to find Internet sites related to this book.
All of the sites on FactHound have been researched by our staff.

Here's how:

1. Visit *www.facthound.com*
2. Type in this special code **0736824502** for age-appropriate sites.
   Or enter a search word related to this book for a more general search.
3. Click on the Fetch It button.

FactHound will fetch the best sites for you!

Index